BJ and the Green Monstah

Tom Dirsa

Illustrations by Matthew McClatchie

Dream Write Publishing Ltd.
P.O. Box 57083 RPO Eastgate
Sherwood Park AB T8A 5L7

http://www.dreamwritepublishing.ca

BJ and the Green Monstah
ISBN # 978-1-927510-76-6

Illustrations by Matthew McClatchie

Major League Baseball trademarks and copyrights are used with permission of Major League Baseball Properties, Inc.

Library and Archives Canada Cataloging in Publication
BJ and the Green Monstah
Dirsa, Thomas (b. September 23, 1941 -)
Leduc AB
McClatchie, Matthew (b. November 21, 1974 -)
Edmonton AB

Printed in the US by CreateSpace

Dedication:

We would like to dedicate this book to all the members of Red Sox Nation who introduce their children and grandchildren to the game of baseball by bringing them to a ballpark.

A special thank you to Major League Baseball and the Red Sox for their willingness to allow us to place this story in one of the great baseball parks in all of baseball with special mention to Kristieanne Karlson from the Major League Baseball office for her understanding, compassion, and assistance in helping us reach our goal of bringing this story to you, the reader.

This is the third story about BJ and his adventures as we all learn about the world of ADHD. He is an active child with tons of questions and often provides a unique response to new information. His reactions to his first baseball game are one such example.

We would like to thank our illustrator, Matthew McClatchie. Matty has worked tirelessly on this project while teaching English as a second language in South Korea. His ability to translate pictures of the mind into reality astounds me every day. To do it thousands of miles away makes his accomplishments even more amazing.

Finally, we want to thank Linda Pedley and every one at Dream Write Publishing Ltd., who truly have the ability to turn our dreams of writing into reality.

"BJ, we have tickets right behind the **Pesky Pole**," Grandpa announces.

"Do we have to sit behind something that's going to be pesky?" asks BJ.

Grandpa laughs. "No, the pole's not pesky. It is named after a famous Red Sox player, who had a few hits that went into the stands near the pole."

"Grandpa? What do you like about baseball?"

"Well, first... because of its long history. It is a game I remember my dad playing, one that I played, and one I watched your dad play... and maybe you will play it in the near future. It is the only game I know where the defense holds the ball. Finally, more than any other sport, it has a place for all types of athletes – tall ones, short ones, thin ones or heavy players can become stars," answers Grandpa.

"One other thing about the game, BJ, is the different games that can be played within the game," Grandpa adds.

"What do you mean?" asks BJ.

"Well, see the man at the plate with a bat?"

"Yes."

"Well, he is called the batter. He has to figure out what kind of pitch the pitcher is going to throw, so he can hit the ball. At the same time, the pitcher needs to figure out which pitch he will throw to make the batter miss the ball," explains Grandpa.

"Does the batter have to swing at every pitch?" asks BJ.

"No, but if the pitcher throws the ball within a certain area, the batter will get a strike. If he gets three strikes, he is out."

"So the batter has to figure out which pitch to swing at? What happens if the ball is not in that certain area, Grandpa?"

"If the pitcher misses four times, it allows the batter to go to first base. It is called a walk," answers Grandpa.

"So... while the batter and the pitcher are playing the pitching game what are the other players doing?" asks BJ.

Grandpa laughs. "They are getting ready to play the ball in case the batter hits it. See the player close to us? He is called the right fielder and see how he is moving closer to the *Pesky Pole*?"

"Yes, I see him moving. Why is he doing that?" inquires BJ.

"Well, the batter is left handed and he just moved his feet, the right fielder knows what the pitcher is going to throw so he is positioning himself where he thinks the batter might hit the ball. See? The other outfielders have all moved closer to us. They think the batter might hit the ball into right field," Grandpa points out.

"Grandpa, where do the players stay when they're not on the field?"

"They sit in that area just behind the baseline. They call it a dugout."

"What is that man doing in the dugout – waving to the players?" BJ asks.

"That man is the manager and he is telling the players in the field where he wants them to play," Grandpa explains.

"What else does he do?"

"Well, he decides who is playing, the batting order, and if there are any changes, he is the one who decides when to make them."

"He is the boss then?"

"I guess you can say that!"

"Grandpa! Is that green thing down on the sidelines the **Green Monstah**?" BJ asks as he points to a large, smiling mascot.

"No." Grandpa chuckles as he shakes his head.

"New Englanders call that big green wall in left field the **Green Monstah**. That green thing on the sidelines is

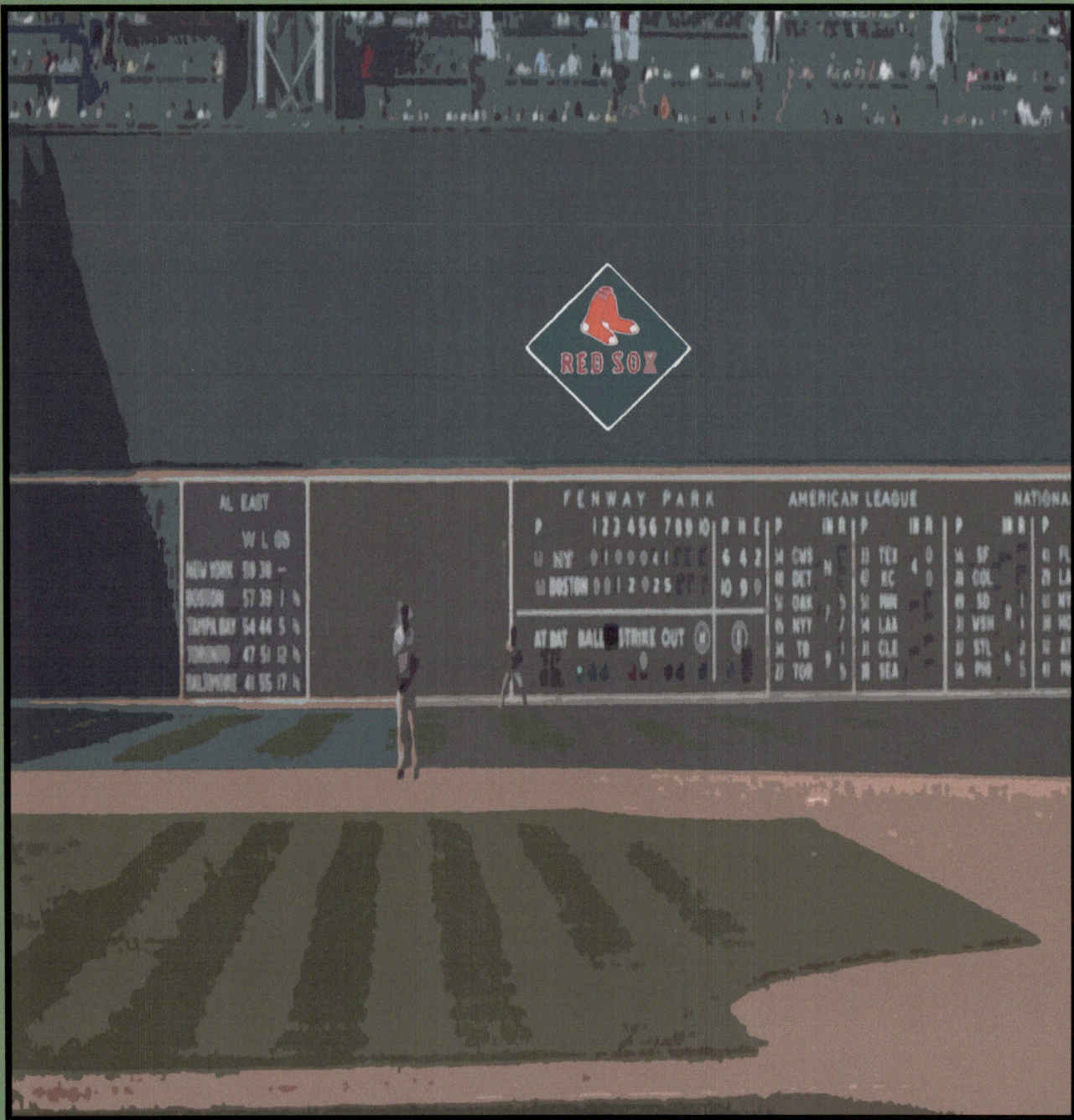

the team mascot. He's **Wally,** and he lives in the **Green Monstah!"**

"Grandpa, why do they call the wall a **Monstah**?"

"Well... if you are a pitcher, the wall feels like it is pressing down on you and a lot of high fly balls – ones that would be an out in another baseball park – end up as a home run. If you are a batter, a line drive hit that would be a home run in another park could end up as a single. The **Monstah** can turn outs into home runs and home runs into singles."

"So, there is nothing to really be scared of, Grandpa?"

"No." Grandpa laughs, and then adds, "Unless you're a rookie."

"Look, Grandpa! All the players are running into the dugout. Is the game over?"

"No, BJ, the pitcher just struck out the batter and

that was the third out. After three outs, the teams switch places. See? The Yankees are now coming out to the field. It is time for the Red Sox to bat. They do that nine times – more if the game is tied after the ninth time," explains Grandpa.

"Grandpa! That batter just hit the ball and it's coming right at us. Can you catch it!" BJ yells, excitedly.

"I'll try!"

Grandpa extends his hands out just in time. "Look! BJ, I got it! Here, now you have a souvenir of your trip to Fenway."

"Was that a home run?" BJ's new acquisition pleases him.

"No, it was a foul ball. It just missed the **Pesky Pole**," answers Grandpa.

"Look! BJ. The runner just stole second base!"

"No, he didn't. It's still there!"

BJ's innocent response prompts more laughter from Grandpa. "No, BJ, a runner can advance a base by stealing it. That means he got there without the help of a hit, a walk, or an error. And, before the catcher could throw him out."

"Grandpa, I'm hungry. What is there to eat?"

"The best ball franks in the world are served right here at Fenway. I'll get two from that vendor and some soft drinks," suggests Grandpa.

"Ball franks? Don't you mean hotdogs, Grandpa?"

"No," replies Grandpa. "Ball franks are much better tasting than any old hotdog. Here, try it."

"You're right! Grandpa, this is delicious!"

"Well, BJ, the game is almost over. So, what did you think of your first baseball game?"

"It was great, Grandpa. I learned that the **Pesky Pole** is not really pesky and that a player can steal but not take anything. I now know that ball franks are great when eaten while watching the Red Sox defeat the Yankees."

BJ smiles proudly, and then continues.

"But... Grandpa? Why is the wall called the **Green Mon-stah** and not mon-ster?"

"Well," explains Grandpa. "That's the way New Englanders often pronounce the name of the wall that has become a big part of their beloved Fenway Park."

BJ smiles again.

"Well... I also learned that the **Green Monster** does not scare kids. Take that, ***Green Mon-stah!***'

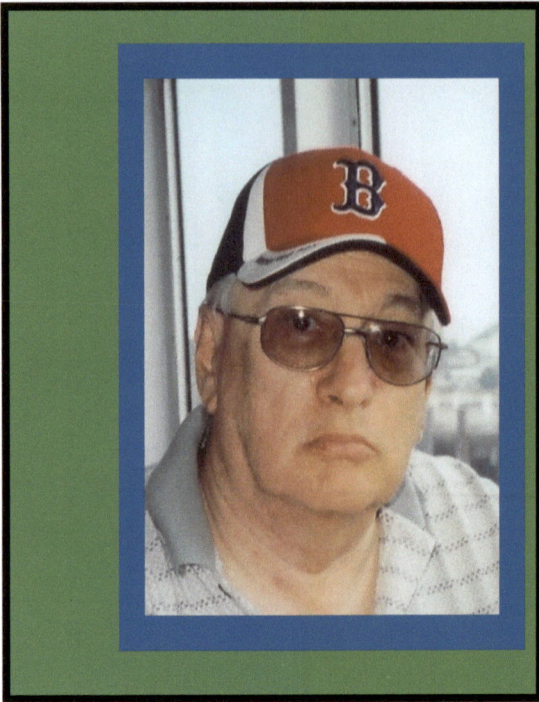

Author - Tom Dirsa

Tom grew up on the tip of Cape Cod in Massachusetts and has been a life long Red Sox fan ever since. After a successful career as a teacher, basketball coach, and school administrator that took him and his wife, Margaret, to New England, Colorado, and Western Canada he retired to Leduc, Alberta, Canada.

Since his retirement, Tom worked on his writing skills as a freelance reporter for a local weekly newspaper, wrote the Junior High Social Studies Preview/Review program for Alberta Distant Learning, was published in a number of national magazines, and has published a number of children's books about a child with ADHD. Currently, he spoke at a number of teachers' conventions while working on his next children's book.

Sweaty Eyes was his first book released in 2014 and follows BJ as he attempts to become a member of a basketball team. In *Fishing Lessons for Grandpa,* BJ learns how to ask for something without asking. You can connect with Tom on Facebook or on his website: http://www.fishinglessonsforgrandpa.com

*****

Illustrator - Matthew McClatchie

Matthew hails from down under and we are so lucky he has dual citizenship and loves spending time in Canada! Matty's work can be found on, and in, a number of Dream Write Publishing books. His ability to create a style and characterization for each book project he is assigned makes his work a true asset to any author's words. His passion for the arts shines through in everything he does. To connect with Matthew, follow him on Facebook and check out his web site: http://tuckerboxdesign.com/

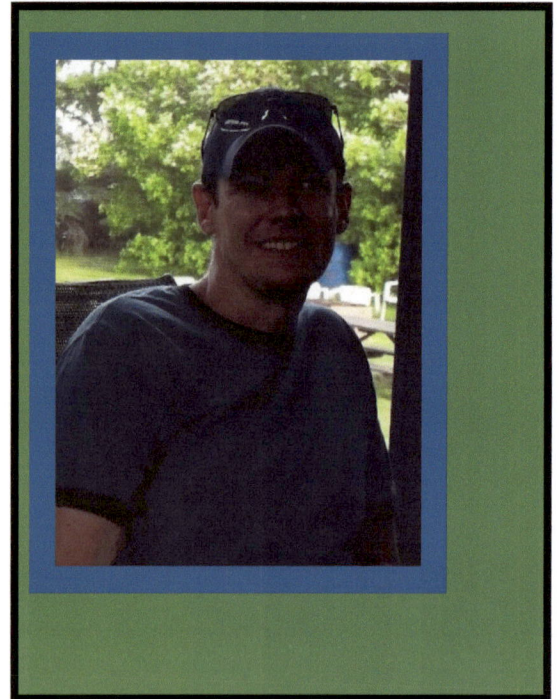

24